LEARN GOOD
ENGLISH

Walter D. Wright

JAMES NISBET & CO. LTD
DIGSWELL PLACE

Published by James Nisbet & Co. Ltd,
Digswell Place, Welwyn Garden City, Herts

0 7202 0931 5

First published 1979

This printing 1979

Printed and bound at William Clowes & Sons Limited,
Beccles and London

Contents

Common or Proper

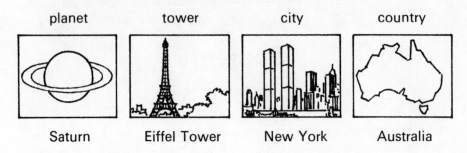

planet	tower	city	country
Saturn	Eiffel Tower	New York	Australia

A word that **names** anything is a **noun**.

The word *planet* can mean any planet. It is called a **common** noun.

But the word *Saturn* refers to one particular planet. It is called a **proper** noun.

Every proper noun begins with a capital letter.

In the same way *tower* can mean any tower, but *Eiffel Tower* is the name of one particular tower. It is a proper noun. Notice that this proper noun is made up of two words. They must each start with a capital letter.

Your own name is a proper noun. Each word in your name must start with a capital letter. Sam Dent

Some words can be either proper nouns or common nouns. It depends on how they are used.

Oxford **Street** is a busy **street**. Tom **Brown** has a **brown** dog.

Write the following words in your ordinary handwriting, putting capitals where they are needed.

ATLANTIC	COUSIN	MOTORWAY	WHITEHALL
TELEVISION	ITALY	NEPTUNE	HOVERCRAFT
VOLCANO	CENTURY	JASON	PARIS
EVEREST	FOOTBALLER	DANUBE	EXAMINATION

Write the following sentences in ordinary handwriting, putting capitals where necessary. Remember that a sentence must start with a capital letter.

1. ST PAUL'S CATHEDRAL IS LONDON'S BEST-KNOWN CATHEDRAL.
2. THE WINE CALLED CHAMPAGNE COMES FROM THE PROVINCE OF CHAMPAGNE IN FRANCE.
3. THE WORLD'S LARGEST LAKE IS LAKE SUPERIOR.
4. THE DAVIS CUP IS A CUP AWARDED FOR TENNIS.
5. THEIR SCHOOL IS THE JOHN TAYLOR MIDDLE SCHOOL.
6. LORD BYRON BECAME A LORD IN 1798.

You also need capitals . . .

1. at the beginning of sentences. Cuckoos sing in May.
2. for the names of months and days. April, Monday, Boxing Day
3. for the first and all important words in the titles of books, plays, etc. Early Days in Britain, The Merchant of Venice, In Search of an Island
4. for adjectives of nationality. He likes French cooking. This is a Persian rug. They speak Welsh.
5. for the pronoun **I**. This is always a capital letter.

Rewrite in ordinary handwriting.

PLYMOUTH IS A FAMOUS PORT AND NAVAL STATION ON PLYMOUTH SOUND IN DEVON. THE PLYM, THE TAVY AND THE TAMAR ARE SOME OF THE RIVERS THAT DRAIN INTO THE SOUND. A BRIDGE BUILT BY BRUNEL CARRIES THE RAILWAY ACROSS THE TAMAR INTO CORNWALL. AT PLYMOUTH HOE DRAKE PLAYED HIS HISTORIC GAME OF BOWLS WHILE WAITING FOR THE SPANISH ARMADA, AND FROM HERE THE PILGRIM FATHERS SET SAIL IN THE MAYFLOWER.

5

Singular or Plural

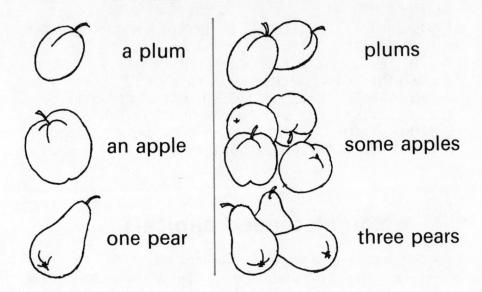

a plum   plums

an apple   some apples

one pear   three pears

A noun that names just one thing is a **singular** noun.
A noun that names more than one thing is a **plural** noun.

To turn most singular nouns into plurals, add **-s** at the end.

      plum—plums   apple—apples   pear—pears

To form the plural of a noun that ends in a hissing or buzzing sound,
we add **-es**.

      dish—dishes   cross—crosses   beach—beaches

If the singular ends in **y** after a consonant, change the **y** into **i** and
add **-es**.

      fly—flies   pony—ponies   baby—babies

But if the singular ends in **y** after a vowel, we do not change the **y**, we
simply add **-s**.

      tray—trays   donkey—donkeys   boy—boys

To turn some singular nouns into plurals, we do not add **s** at all, but we change the vowel sound.

tooth—teeth   man—men   mouse—mice

Words that end in **f** or **fe** usually change the **f** into **v** before adding **-s** or **-es**.

shelf—shelves   wolf—wolves   knife—knives

But words that end in **ff** or **ffe** usually just add **-s**.

cliff—cliffs   cuff—cuffs   giraffe—giraffes

Complete the following plurals.

1. Nought____ and cross____
2. Cup____ and saucer____
3. Plate____ and dish____
4. Carton____ and box____
5. Actor____ and actress____
6. Jeans with big patch____
7. Prefix____ and suffix____
8. Hiss____ and buzz____

Complete these sentences.

1. Roy had a collection of moths and _____. (butterfly)
2. _____ are protected birds. (osprey)
3. The lawn was white with _____. (daisy)
4. Boats were moored along all the _____. (quay)
5. The information desk will answer your _____. (query)
6. They took no notice of his shouts and _____. (cry)
7. We can lift heavy things by means of _____. (pulley)
8. They picked _____ for jam. (raspberry)
9. In autumn the _____ of many trees turn yellow. (leaf)
10. Tower blocks have many _____. (storey)

The spelling of unusual plurals can be found in most dictionaries. Using your dictionary if necessary, give the plural of these examples.

1. A long striped scarf
2. A woman in a red jersey
3. An extinct volcano
4. A giraffe and a zebra
5. A cockatoo with a fine crest
6. Seagulls nesting on a cliff
7. Bring your wife and family
8. A cart drawn by an ox
9. A turkey and a goose
10. An adult and a child
11. The chief wore his uniform.
12. A sheep and a deer grazing

This is a Sentence—

You will go to prison for three years.

In grammar a **sentence** is a group of words that make complete sense.

A sentence begins with a capital letter and ends with a full stop.

The dog is barking.　　I went to town.　　The gate was shut.

A sentence can be a question—What did you eat? or it can be an order—Stop teasing the dog! In these cases a question mark or an exclamation mark acts as a full stop.

Sentences can be very long or they can be as short as two words; but each sentence must make complete sense.

Write each of the following passages in four sentences.

1. LIZARDS CANNOT STAND COLD WEATHER THEY HAVE SCALY BODIES AND ARE FOUND IN WARM LANDS THERE ARE HUNDREDS OF DIFFERENT KINDS THE LARGEST OF ALL IS MORE THAN THREE METRES LONG
2. FLINT IS VERY HARD STONE IT HAS SHARP EDGES PREHISTORIC MEN USED IT TO MAKE AXES THEY ALSO MADE ARROW HEADS OF IT

—but This is Not

baking a cake

I like

Who is

is fun

?

Try

looks easy

The words **baking a cake** do not tell us anything definite. They do not make a sentence. They make a **phrase**.

A phrase is a group of words that belong together but do not make a complete statement.

A phrase does not contain a full verb. **baking** is only part of a verb.

Use the clues in the picture with the phrase **baking a cake** to make five complete sentences. Be sure to start each sentence with a capital letter and end it with a full stop or a question mark.

Phrases often start with a preposition:

on the train   under the sea   into the bath

Say which of the following are sentences and which are phrases.

1. The sun is shining.
2. Singing a new song
3. These are young leopards.
4. With the lion cubs
5. Hoping to win a prize

6. Was he hoping to win?
7. Over the rainbow
8. On the sidelines
9. They lined the way.
10. Before going to sleep

Building a Sentence

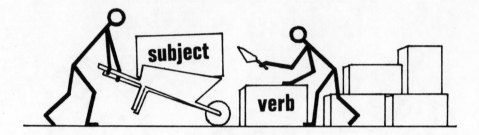

In order to build a sentence you need two things—a **subject** and a **verb**. They lay the foundation. Any other information is built up on them.

Look at these sentences:

The children play on the swing.   The wind blows.
The man was laughing loudly.   He went away.

In each sentence there is a naming part and a doing part.

Naming

The part that *names* the person or thing we are talking about is the **subject**. The subject is usually a noun or a word standing for a noun. We can divide our sentences like this:

Naming (subject)	**Doing** (predicate)
The children	play on the swing.
The wind	blows.
The man	was laughing loudly.
He	went away.

Supply a subject for each of the following sentences.

1. _____ went for a long walk.
2. _____ picked basketfuls of raspberries.
3. _____ won the heavyweight boxing title.
4. _____ painted this picture. _____ won a prize.
5. _____ visited Jamaica in the royal yacht Britannia.
6. _____ are visiting France next holidays.
7. _____ were caught with the contraband.
8. _____ can go to the library. _____ are going to the Sports Centre.
9. _____ forgot to leave us any milk.
10. _____ went out and left us in the dark.

Doing

A word that tells us what the subject *does* is a **verb**.

Birds *fly*.   Men *work*.   The wind *blows*.   I *run*.

These action verbs are easy to recognize.

There are also verbs of *being*.

I *am*   Men *are*   The dog *is*

They need something added before they make a complete statement.

I am happy. Men are wise. The dog is friendly.

Complete each of the following sentences with an interesting predicate.

1. The spaceship _____
2. Thousands of people _____
3. The volcano _____
4. The secret agent _____
5. Dozens of white butterflies _____
6. Land-based helicopters _____
7. Police with tracker dogs _____
8. Tourists from all over the world _____

11

They Must Agree

The man works.
One hammer **is** heavy.

The men work.
Two hammers **are** heavy.

If the subject of a sentence is singular, the verb that goes with it must be singular. If the subject is plural, the verb must be plural to match.

Are you sure of these verbs? People often make mistakes with them.

Singular	Plural
is	are
was	were
has	have

Complete these sentences with the correct verbs.

1. Coconuts _____ on palm trees. grows/grow
2. These cherries _____ very sweet. is/are
3. The young robin _____ a speckled breast. has/have
4. We _____ going home from school. was/were
5. Red Indians _____ in North America. lives/live

The Object

The man painted the wall.

The man is the subject. **Painted** is the verb. Ask the question *painted what?* The answer is **the wall**. **The wall** is the object of **painted**.

In many sentences the subject and verb must have an object. Pick out the subject, verb and object in these examples.

1. Lightning struck the tree.
2. Barry drove the tractor.
3. The searchers found Tom and Benny.
4. Valerie dropped her plate of soup.
5. The boy flew his model aeroplane.

In which of the following sentences does the verb take an object? Give the verb and the object.

1. The aeroplane flew high above the clouds.
2. The pilot flew the hijacked plane to Rome.
3. She spread butter on the bread.
4. The stain spread across the ceiling.

Instead of a Noun

He visited **her**.

She visited **him**.

Personal pronouns are words used instead of nouns. A noun remains the same whether it is the subject or the object of a verb, but most of the personal pronouns have to change when they are the object. The exceptions are *it* and *you* which remain the same.

Subject	Object	Subject	Object
a. I	me	*f.* it	it
b. he	him	*g.* you	you
c. she	her		
d. we	us		
e. they	them		

Supply the correct form of the pronouns indicated.

1. *d* saw *c*.
2. *b* teaches *a*.
3. *f* hurt *g*.
4. *c* told *b*.
5. *a* chased *e*.
6. *e* know *d*.

14

He to her. . . . She to him

Like a verb, a preposition can have an object. So a personal pronoun after a preposition must be in the objective form.

Come with me.   Sweets for him

Sitting beside her   Floating above them

Using the table on the opposite page, replace the letters with personal pronouns.

1. *a* helped *g*.
2. *e* warned *a*.
3. *d* heard from *b*.
4. *b* wrote to *g*.
5. *g* suspected *e*.
6. *a* caught *f* from *c*.
7. *e* sided with *b* against *d*.
8. *f* arrived before *c*.
9. *d* shared *f* amongst *e*.
10. Keep *f* between *g* and *a*.

In the exercise below, put personal pronouns for the words in italics. Watch for those following a preposition.

1. *Alex* visited *Tim and Mark*.
2. *Nicola* came with *Patsy and me*.
3. *Tim and Mark* saw *Alex*.
4. *Rose* looked at *Mary*.
5. *Tom* talked about *you and me*.
6. *Kathy* visited *Nicola*.
7. *The book* was under *Bob*.
8. *Mary* waited for *Jane*.
9. *Kathy and I* came after *Tom*.
10. *Alex* went without *Tim and Rose*.

To, Two, Too

To   means *towards*, or is part of a verb.
Two   is a number.
Too   suggests degree, or it can mean *also*.

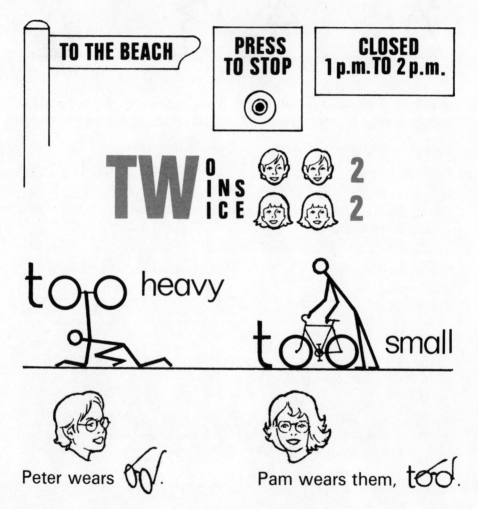

TO THE BEACH

PRESS
TO STOP

CLOSED
1 p.m. TO 2 p.m.

TW**O** **INS** **ICE** 2 2

t**oo** heavy

t**oo** small

Peter wears ☍.   Pam wears them, t**oo**.

Of or Off

Of means *belonging to*, *made from*, or it links two words.

The teeth of a tiger

A bunch of flowers

Proud of success

Off means *away*, *away from*, and suggests movement.

Fall off the ladder

The lid is off.

A long way off

Complete these examples with *of* or *off*.
1. Keep _____ the grass.
2. It was _____ the beaten track.
3. A cup _____ hot soup
4. The box was made _____ ivory.
5. They set _____ for Holland.
6. The aeroplane was ready to take _____.
7. She was glad _____ an extra coat.

Links in a Chain

When two sentences are *closely related* they can be joined into one sentence by the word **and**.

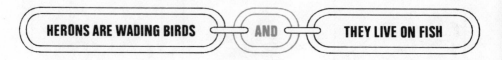

When two sentences are *contrasted* they can be joined into one sentence by the word **but**.

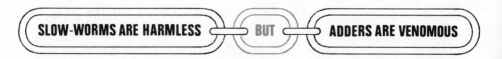

Notice that the two parts of the sentence are of equal importance.

Because they are *joining* words, **and** and **but** are called **conjunctions**.

Using **and** or **but**, join the following pairs of sentences.

1. One of the men was a carpenter. The other was a plumber.
2. Ted passed in six subjects. Michael passed in only one.
3. The flying fish glides above the sea. It cannot really fly.
4. The cock pheasant has brilliant plumage. The hen is very drab.
5. Jane was painting. Judy was doing a crossword.
6. Cats see well at night. They cannot see in pitch darkness.
7. Whales live in the sea. They are not fish.
8. Nightingales are best heard at night. They also sing in the daytime.
9. Monkeys live in trees. They eat bananas and other fruit.
10. Frogs can stay under water a long time. They have to come up for air.

More Joining Words

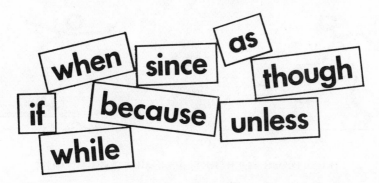

The conjunctions above are used to link the principal sentence with a sentence of less importance. Dependent sentences add interest and information by telling, for instance, how, when, where or why a thing is done.

Using one of the conjunctions above, join the following sentences.

1. The doctor was called. The boy was badly hurt.
2. The headmaster said I could go. I had finished my work.
3. They kept on looking. There was no hope of finding him.
4. He came to see us. He had promised.
5. She waited outside. I talked to the doctor.

Complete the sentences below. Notice that the dependent clause can be put before the principal sentence.

1. The sea birds were dying because _____.
2. Put your coat on before _____.
3. We must get more bread since _____.
4. While _____, three No. 7 buses went by.
5. Unless _____ you will not pass your test.
6. When _____ we can play rounders.
7. As _____ he slipped and fell.
8. If _____ we shall have a good crop of apples.

Two in One

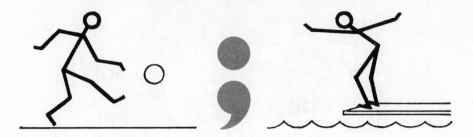

Tim likes football; I prefer swimming.

A semicolon ; can be used to join two closely related or strongly contrasted sentences into one. The word following the semicolon does not have a capital letter (unless it is a proper noun).

In each of the following examples use a semicolon to join the two sentences into one.

1. The Indian rhinoceros has a single horn. The African rhinoceros has two.
2. Platinum is a very heavy metal. No acid affects it.
3. Cactus plants can live in hot dry places. They store moisture in their stems.
4. The earth takes a year to go round the sun. Pluto takes 248 years.

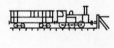

Pause for a comma   stay longer at a semicolon   stop at a full stop

Asking or Telling

Does it need a question mark?

A

B

Simon asked how much the plant was.

In **A** Simon is actually *asking* the question. A question mark is needed.

In **B** someone is *telling* about Simon's question. It is a statement. No question mark is needed.

Write out these sentences, adding a full stop or question mark.

1. Would you like some lemonade
2. She asked me if I would like some lemonade
3. Guess how old I am
4. How old am I
5. What time is it
6. I want to know what time it is
7. I wonder if I can afford it
8. Do you think I can afford it
9. Ask someone where the post office is
10. Can you tell me where the post office is

21

A Pageful of Plurals

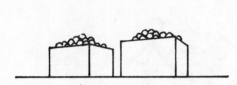

Two boxes full   Two boxfuls

For two **boxes full** of apples you need two boxes.

For two **boxfuls** of apples you can use one box and fill it twice.

A **boxful** is a measure. It is what a box will hold. Notice that **boxful** has only one **l**. The plural is **boxfuls**.

Complete these phrases, using the clues in brackets.

1. Two _____ of sugar (spoon)
2. Four _____ of sand (bucket)
3. Three _____ of nuts (hand)
4. Ten _____ of sticks (arm)
5. Six _____ of earth (spade)
6. A few _____ of food (mouth)
7. Two _____ of soup (bowl)
8. Several _____ of peas (basket)
9. Two _____ of gold dust (fist)

A Mouthful of Fudge

2 cupfuls of sugar   2 tablespoonfuls of butter

1 cupful of milk   1 teaspoonful of vanilla

Melt them together in a saucepan and boil for 15 minutes. Remove from the heat and beat until nearly thick. Pour into a buttered dish.

22

Rather Different

 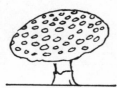 

Some words, especially those borrowed from foreign languages, have unusual plurals. Only by learning them and using them do you come to know them.

In the phrases below, choose the correct singular or plural. Use a dictionary if you are not sure.

1. A poisonous *fungus/fungi* like a toadstool
2. Euston and other London *terminus/termini*
3. A *phenomenon/phenomena* like a mirage
4. A snakes-and-ladders board and a *die/dice*
5. Brochures from all the travel *bureau/bureaux*
6. The *radius/radii* of two circles
7. Grubs called *larva/larvae* which turn into moths
8. Travelling on camels to a distant *oasis/oases*
9. Broadcasting through the different *medium/media*
10. A chemical *formula/formulae* such as H_2SO_4
11. Hundreds of *gladiolus/gladioli* in flower
12. A *stratum/strata* of coal between two *stratum/strata* of rock

Penny has two plurals—**pennies** and **pence**. Either is right.

Singular Subject, Singular Verb

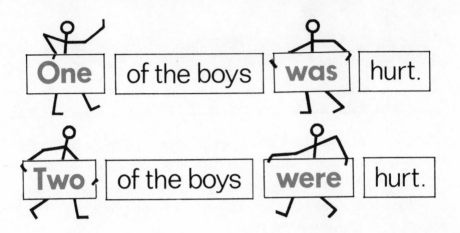

In a sentence the verb must agree with the subject. *But* make sure which word is the subject. In the first sentence above the subject is not *boys*, but *one* of the boys. The noun *one* is singular, so the verb must be singular to agree.

In the following sentences, choose the verb that agrees with the subject. To help you decide on the subject, the first ones have been put in italics.

1. *One* of my rabbits _____ died. has/have
2. *A case* of tools _____ missing. is/are
3. *The cracks* in this wall _____ mending. needs/need
4. The design of these skirts _____ Austrian. is/are
5. A box full of apples _____ in the corner. was/were
6. Showers of rain turning to snow _____ expected. is/are
7. A ring with several diamonds _____ more. costs/cost
8. The weather in all regions _____ likely to improve. is/are

24

Two singular nouns joined by *and* make a plural subject which must be followed by a plural verb.

Janet *and* Rosie *are* making toffee.
Michael *and* I *were* playing chess.

But   Janet *as well as* Rosie *is* making toffee.
Janet *but not* Rosie *is* making toffee.

Each and Every One

When we use the words **each** or **every** we are talking of each separate one of a group, so the subject is singular and is followed by a singular verb.

Each man *was* asked his name.
Each of the men *was* asked his name.
Every girl *is* wearing a beret.
Every one of the girls *is* wearing a beret.

But   *All* the men *were* asked their names.
All the girls *are* wearing berets.

Write the following sentences correctly.

1. Each of these boxes _____ old coins.   contains/contain
2. Every one of my photographs _____ spoiled.   is/are
3. Each of the boys _____ to make _____ own _____.
   has/have   his/their   bed/beds
4. Both Roger and John _____ joining the Navy.   is/are
5. Each tin of humbugs _____ a hundred sweets.   contains/contain
6. Every one _____ _____ own idea of fair play.
   has/have   his/their

25

Group Words

These are seven stars.   This is a constellation.

The word **star** is singular. The plural is **stars**. But if you think of a number of stars as one particular group or pattern, you call the group a **constellation**. The word **constellation** is singular. It takes a singular verb.

In the same way, we say

> Father, Mother and the children *were* all ill,

but

> The whole family *was* ill.

Other group words are   team   fleet   audience   class.

These group words are called **collective** nouns. A collective noun is singular. It takes a singular verb.

Give the group names used for these things.

1. A _____ of bees   4. A _____ of wolves
2. A _____ of starlings   5. A _____ of mackerel
3. A _____ of cows   6. A _____ of lions

In the following examples, choose the correct verb.

1. The choir _____ singing an anthem.   was/were
2. The regiment _____ posted overseas.   is/are
3. The crowd _____ against the barrier.   push/pushes
4. The flock of sheep _____ driven by dogs.   is/are
5. The class _____ been visiting the zoo.   has/have

26

Tense Tells When

Past **Present** **Future**

We use the **present tense** for something that is happening now.

The picture hangs on the wall at present.

We use the **past tense** for something that has already happened.

The picture hung on the wall last year.

We use the **future tense** for something that will happen in the time ahead.

The picture will hang there next year.

Be careful not to mix the tenses when you are giving an account of something.

Below is part of a letter about a seaside holiday. Write it out, first in the past tense, then in the present tense, using the right verbs from the numbered list.

Each day after breakfast we ____1___ down to the harbour. If the tide ____2___ out we ____3___ games, ____4___ castles, ____5___ in shallow pools and ____6___ to fishermen working on their boats. When the tide

27

_____7_____ in, I _____8_____ a long swim, while Linda and Timothy _____9_____ around in the rubber dinghy. We _____10_____ to stay at the harbour for lunch, and Mother sometimes _____11_____ her lunch down too. We _____12_____ stay by the water for the whole day.

1. went	go	7. is	was
2. was	is	8. enjoyed	enjoy
3. played	play	9. sculled	scull
4. build	built	10. like	liked
5. paddle	paddled	11. brought	brings
6. talked	talk	12. can	could

Mistakes are most often made in the use of the past tense. Verbs are expressed by

1. the complete verb in one word—We **ran**.

2. a group of words made up of helping verbs together with a participle—We **were running**.

It is a bad mistake to use a past participle as a complete verb, or to use a complete verb with a helping word as if it were a participle. You can see some of these mistakes below.

Do **not** say	Say
I seen him.	I *saw* him.
She done it.	She *did* it.
The pipes were froze.	The pipes *were frozen*.
They come last week.	They *came* last week.
Have you forgot?	*Have* you *forgotten*?
The cup was broke.	The cup *was broken*.
We been to town.	We *have been* to town.
We all sung folk songs.	We all *sang* folk songs.

28

In each pair of words below the first one is the complete past tense and the second is the past participle. Choose the right one to complete each unfinished sentence. Use the past participles as partners for the helping verbs given in the sentences.

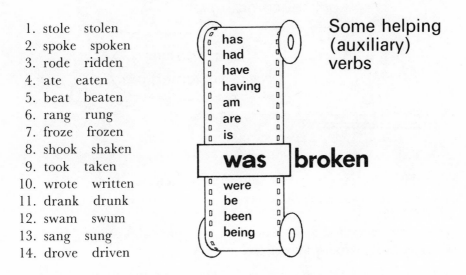

1. stole   stolen
2. spoke   spoken
3. rode   ridden
4. ate   eaten
5. beat   beaten
6. rang   rung
7. froze   frozen
8. shook   shaken
9. took   taken
10. wrote   written
11. drank   drunk
12. swam   swum
13. sang   sung
14. drove   driven

Some helping (auxiliary) verbs

has
had
have
having
am
are
is

was **broken**

were
be
been
being

1. He _____ a watch.   The watch was _____.
2. French was _____.   I _____ French to him.
3. They _____ camels.   Camels can be _____.
4. They _____ berries.   They had _____ berries.
5. He was being _____.   Did you _____ him?
6. Will the bell be _____?   He _____ the bell.
7. The water was _____.   The water _____.
8. The house _____.   The house was _____.
9. I _____ a photo.   A photo has been _____.
10. It was _____ in ink.   She _____ it in ink.
11. I _____ my tea.   I have _____ my tea.
12. We have _____ ashore.   We _____ ashore.
13. Hymns were _____.   They _____ a hymn.
14. He had never _____ a car.   He _____ the car.

Teaching and Learning

The skiing instructor is a **teacher**; he **teaches**.
The boy is a **learner**; he **learns**.

Teaching is **giving** instruction.
Learning is **getting** knowledge or skill.

It is wrong to say that someone *learns* you. Someone may *teach* you, but you must *learn*.

In the following sentences, replace the dash with one of these words:

learn, learned, learning, teach, teaches, taught.

1. Who _____ you to swim?
2. Please _____ me how to do that trick.
3. I want to _____ how to play the piano.
4. We are _____ French. Mr Hassall _____ us.
5. It was a mistake, but I _____ my lesson.
6. That will _____ you to tease the cat!
7. My mother _____ me the alphabet.
8. She says I _____ it easily.
9. He _____ them all about sailing.
10. They have to _____ the rules.

Not Nothing = Something

The man on the left caught nothing. It would be a bad mistake to say **He didn't catch nothing.** If he did *not* catch *nothing* he must have caught *something*.

In the same way, **There was never no one in the house** means that there was always someone in the house.

Using one word from A or B, complete the sentences below so that they have a **negative** meaning.

A   nowhere   nobody   none

(Do not use any of these with not, n't, never, hardly, scarcely.)

B   any   anyone   anything   anybody   anywhere

1. We didn't buy _____ from him.
2. There was never _____ in the house.
3. Remember to go _____ near the cliffs.
4. This is a secret. Tell _____ what I have said.
5. I can't find my racket _____.
6. They had hardly _____ fine weather.
7. We wanted bacon but the butcher had _____.
8. Hasn't _____ seen my watch?

Two, or More than Two?

He is tall.   He is the taller.   He is the tallest.

Adjectives have three degrees.

When speaking of 1 person or thing we use the **positive** form.

When speaking of 2 persons or things we use the **comparative** form.

When speaking of more than 2 we use the **superlative** form.

To turn a short adjective into the comparative form, add **-er**.
To turn a short adjective into the superlative form, add **-est**.

Positive	Comparative	Superlative
tall	taller	tallest
dark	darker	darkest
heavy	heavier	heaviest
brave	braver	bravest

Long adjectives remain unchanged, but have **more** or **most** before them to form comparative and superlative.

beautiful fragrant	more beautiful more fragrant	most beautiful most fragrant

In the following examples, replace each dash with the comparative or superlative form of the adjective in brackets.

1. Which is the _____, the bus or the train?   (quick)
2. The _____ animal of all is the whale.   (large)
3. Which is the _____, a mile or a kilometre?   (long)
4. Use either nylon or hemp; nylon is _____ than hemp. (strong)
5. Mirror, mirror on the wall, who is the _____ of them all?   (fair)
6. Which is the _____, copper or lead?   (valuable)
7. Who is the _____ of the English poets?   (famous)
8. Both girls are clever, but Jill is the _____.   (intelligent)

Some adjectives are irregular

Positive	Comparative	Superlative
good bad much little	better worse more less	best worst most least

9. Of the two boys, Jeremy is the _____ player.   (good)
10. Five girls had bad results, but Betty's were the _____.   (bad)
11. Of the four cars in the crash, ours was the _____ damaged.   (little)
12. His dog is _____ tempered than mine.   (bad)

Lie or Lay

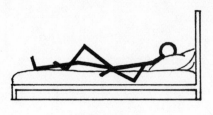

to lie   to lay

To **lie** is to be at rest, or stretched out in a horizontal position. Other parts of this verb are **lies**, **lying**, **lay** and **lain** . . . (but *not* laid).

He *lies* in bed.   He is *lying* in bed.

He *lay* in bed all day.   He was *lying* in bed.

He has *lain* there all day.   They will *lie* in bed.

To **lay** needs an object. It means to put it down, to place it or to set it. Other parts of this verb are **lays**, **laying** and **laid**.

The hen *lays* eggs.   She is *laying* an egg.

She *laid* one yesterday.   She was *laying* it yesterday.

She has *laid* six this week.   She will *lay* one tomorrow.

Complete these sentences. Be very careful not to muddle the two verbs.

1. He _____ down to get his breath.
2. The snow was _____ very thick and deep.
3. The builders have already _____ the foundations.
4. He has _____ unconscious for a week.
5. He didn't _____ the blame on me.
6. He _____ the blame on the boy next door.

34

7. If you are tired, go and _____ down.
8. We cleared the grate and _____ the fire.
9. How long has the wreck _____ on the sea bed?
10. Workmen are busy _____ a new carpet.

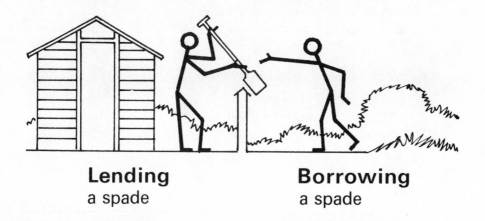

Lending
a spade

Borrowing
a spade

Complete the following sentences.

1. He asked if I would _____ him my pen.
2. It is raining hard. Let me _____ you an umbrella.
3. She had to _____ money for the bus fare.
4. I _____ a lot of books from the library.
5. They _____ us their caravan for a holiday.
6. I don't like _____. I would rather go without.

 Ask for the **loan** of a spade.

35

Seeing Clear **ly**

> **Adjectives** describe or limit **nouns**.
> > a **pretty** girl
> > **one** tree
>
> **Adverbs** tell us more about **verbs**.
> > ran **fast**
> > sang **loudly**

Adverbs modify verbs, adjectives and other adverbs.

> The bell rang *loudly*.
> You must come *now*.   (verbs)
> He looked *there*.

> You are *too* noisy.
> Don't be *so* silly   (adjectives)
> She was *very* careful.

> It was *very* well done.   (adverbs)
> That went *quite* quickly

We form many adverbs by adding **-ly** to the adjective

> sweet—sweetly   open—openly   sure—surely

but take care with adjectives ending in **-al**. Don't cut them short.

> vertical—verti**cally**   accidental—acciden**tally**
> incidental—inciden**tally**   eventual—eventu**ally**

36

Sometimes the adjective and the adverb are the same.

fast   early   late   hard   weekly   near   far

A weekly paper is published weekly.
The fast train goes fast.

Always be careful to use the adjective with a noun and the adverb with a verb.
Complete the sentences with the correct form of the word in brackets.

1. A _____ march is played _____. (quick)
2. On a _____ day we can see the hills _____. (clear)
3. An _____ person will think _____. (intelligent)
4. He made a _____ movement. He moved _____. (sudden)
5. He added _____, so he got the _____ answer. (wrong)

 **Good** is an adjective.   A good hit
Well is the adverb.   He hit it well.

continually breaking windows
(very often)

ticking continuously
(without stopping)

37

Owners and Users

 a **bird's** nest

 **birds'** nests

a **man's** tie

a **man's** ties

men's ties

The pictures show how apostrophes point out the owners or users of things.

The nest belongs to one bird . . . apostrophe after *bird*

The nests belong to two birds . . . apostrophe after *birds*

The tie belongs to one man . . . apostrophe after *man*

The ties belong to one man . . . apostrophe after *man*

The ties belong to two men . . . apostrophe after *men*

In the following examples pick out the owners or users. Take particular notice of what comes *before* the apostrophe.

1. The cows' tails
2. The cow's horns
3. The footballer's boots
4. The footballers' stockings
5. The nurses' hostel
6. The nurse's patients
7. The ponies' hooves
8. The pony's ears
9. The foxes' cubs
10. The fox's brush
11. My uncle's dogs
12. My uncles' stables

Filling the Gaps

The notice says **Do not** but Mother says **Don't**.

In a business letter you would write **I have already paid**; in speaking you could say **I've already paid**.

When letters are left out like this, an apostrophe is needed to take their place. If a group of two or three letters is dropped, one apostrophe is sufficient. The shortened word is run on to the one before it.

> do not ⟶ do n't ⟶ don't
> I have ⟶ I 've ⟶ I've

Shorten the words in italics into single words, putting in apostrophes where they should go.

1. *What is* that?
2. You *must not* go.
3. Our *team has* won.
4. *They are* both well.
5. *There is* no soap.
6. It *does not* matter.
7. The eggs *are not* fresh.
8. I *can not* swim.
9. *They have* just come.
10. *We shall* write to you.
11. *You would* never guess.
12. *I shall* have some tea.
13. He *does not* smoke.
14. *How is* that?

Don't Pepper Them

Some people scatter apostrophes as if they were shaking them from a pepper-pot. Notices often advertise **Tea's, Ice's, Potatoe's** or **Snack's.** These are wrong.

> Apostrophes are used *only*
> 1. to show possession   Jim's pen
> 2. to show that letters have been left out   don't

Ordinary plurals do not need apostrophes.

Copy these notices, putting in apostrophes where necessary.

1. Cadburys Chocolates
2. You cant buy better butter
3. Smiths Crisps
4. Childrens playground
5. Dont miss these bargains!
6. Girls dresses
7. Cafe opens at 12 oclock
8. One hours delay
9. Cars parked at customers own risk
10. Prices down for two weeks
11. This weeks offer
12. Waiting limited to two hours
13. Closed for two weeks holiday

40

A Matter of Place

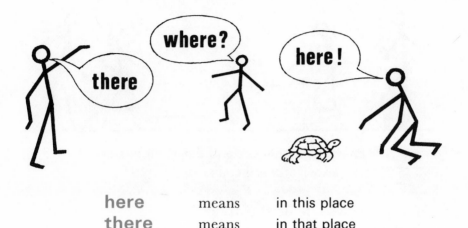

here	means	in this place
there	means	in that place
where	means	in what place?

The words **there** and **their** are often confused. So are **where** and **were**. **There** and **where** are concerned with place, and contain the word **here**. If you remember that you will know which word to use.

Complete the examples. They all have to do with *place*.

1. Look over _____.
2. _____ are you going?
3. _____ we are again!
4. Is _____ any room?
5. _____ am I?
6. I know _____ to go.
7. _____ goes my balloon.
8. _____ is our gate.
9. I'll find _____ they hide.
10. You can't stay _____.

hither	means	to this place
thither	means	to that place
whither	means	to what place?
hence	means	from this place
thence	means	from that place
whence	means	from what place?

41

Either, neither

This chair **is** suitable . . . and this chair **is** suitable.
Either of these chairs **is** suitable.

Either means **one or the other**.
Neither means **not one**, **not the other**.

Either and **neither** are therefore singular, and must take singular verbs.

A word like a pronoun or a possessive adjective standing for **either** or **neither** must also be singular to agree with it.

Neither of the purses **has** any money in **it**.

In the following sentences, choose the correct words.

1. Neither of my brothers *like/likes* yogurt.
2. Tell me if either of these buses *go/goes* to Prestford.
3. Neither of the coats *was/were* long enough.
4. *Has/Have* either of the teams arrived yet?
5. Either Clare or Emma *is/are* to be captain.
6. *Have/Has* either of my shoes any mud on *it/them*?
7. Neither of the workmen *has/have* brought *his/their* tools.
8. I hope neither of the girls *loses/lose her/their* way.
9. Either Simon or Alan *was/were* playing *his/their* guitar.
10. *Do/Does* either of you know what time it is?

Either, or . . . Neither, nor

Either milk **or** cocoa, please

Neither coffee **nor** tea, thank you

Or follows **either**.　　**Nor** follows **neither**.

Following this rule, complete these sentences.

1. She can neither swim _____ skate.
2. They looked for either a lay-by _____ a car park.
3. Neither Sally _____ Sam has taken the test.
4. Either red _____ orange will look well, but neither green _____ blue will do.
5. It is neither iron _____ steel, but either copper _____ brass.

Sharing a Cake

between
two persons

among
three or more persons

43

Fewer than . . . Less than

many apples   fewer apples   **but**   much flour   less flour

Many and **fewer** refer to number—things you can count.
Much and **less** refer to amount—quantities you measure.

We say: Fewer than twenty . . . fewer boys than girls

but: Less than a pound . . . less butter than sugar.

Similarly   much timber . . . many trees
               less sport . . . fewer games
               much bird life . . . many birds

Put *less* or *fewer* before each of the words below.

1. money, coins
2. traffic, cars
3. burglaries, crime
4. showers, rain
5. help, helpers

6. oranges, fruit
7. industry, factories
8. wind, gales
9. cattle, meat
10. food, sandwiches

Put *much* or *many* before each of the words below.

1. houses, accommodation
2. foliage, leaves
3. ships, shipping
4. bread, loaves
5. hours, time

6. mutton, sheep
7. worries, anxiety
8. expense, bills
9. news, newspapers
10. men, manpower

No Apostrophe Needed

Something which is **our** property is **ours**.
If you say

our cat	**his** game
their house	**her** garden
my hat	**your** fault

the bold words are *adjectives*. They stand before a noun.

If you say

The cat is **ours**.	The game is **his**.
The house is **theirs**.	The garden is **hers**.
The hat is **mine**.	The fault is **yours**.

you turn the adjective into a *pronoun.* Pronouns do *not* take apostrophes.

In the following sentences, choose the right pronoun from the illustration to replace the words in italics.

1. This hamster is *my property*.
2. The album is *owned by him*.
3. The large room is *for your use*.
4. The bats are *their property*.
5. Jill's dog is a terrier; *our dog* is a spaniel.
6. *Who is the owner of* that castle?
7. That bed is *for her use*.

Get These Right

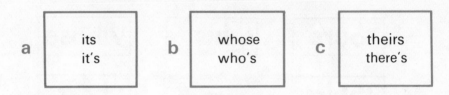

a	its it's	**b**	whose who's	**c**	theirs there's

There is no need to get these words wrong, though many people do muddle them.

The apostrophe here shows that something has been left out.

It's is short for **It is** or **It has** . . . It's gone.

Who's is short for **Who is** or **Who has** . . . Who's coming?

There's is short for **There is** or **There has** . . . There's no soap.

Its is a possessive adjective like *his* or *her* . . . The cat opened its eyes.

Whose is a possessive adjective . . . Whose coat is this?
or a possessive pronoun . . . Whose is this coat?

Theirs is a possessive pronoun . . . The magazines are theirs.

In the following exercises, supply the right missing words from the appropriate box. Use an apostrophe only if something has been left out.

a

1. The scorpion has a sting in _____ tail.
2. _____ a long way to Tipperary.
3. Tell me when _____ ready.
4. _____ never too late to mend.
5. The fox found _____ way back to _____ den.
6. _____ a swan with two cygnets on _____ back.

b

1. _____ umbrella is this?
2. _____ been using my paintbrush?
3. I know a boy _____ uncle is an astronaut.
4. _____ going to watch the eclipse?
5. _____ is that old car?
6. That is the girl _____ cat won a prize.

c

1. _____ been a thunderstorm.
2. Are the coat hangers ours or _____ ?
3. Our train was on time, but _____ was late.
4. _____ no point in waiting any longer.
5. See if _____ any soup left.
6. This is all our luggage. They took _____ with them.

In the following exercise, turn the words in italics into one word.

1. If *it is* worth doing at all, *it is* worth doing well.
2. *Who is* going to come down for a swim?
3. *There is* a quick way of working out that sum.
4. Do you know *who has* been selected?
5. He says *there is* no room for any more passengers.
6. *It has* stopped raining so the match can be played.

Still no apostrophe

Yours truly
Yours sincerely
Yours faithfully
Yours affectionately

47

Short Cuts

A place where scientific experiments are done is called a **laboratory**; but when you are talking or writing quickly it is easier to call it a **lab**. **Telephone** is often shortened to **phone** in conversation; but it is usually printed in full.

Can you complete the words in these dictionary definitions?

1. **gym**_____........A room for physical training.
2. **ref**_____ ....A person who acts as judge in a game.
3. **pop**_____ ....Liked or done by many people.
4. **amp**_____........A unit of electric current.
5. **vet**_____ ....A person who treats sick animals.
6. **pram**_____.......A baby's carriage.
7. _____**flu**_____......A feverish cold.

Many common titles are abbreviated.

Mr, **Mrs**, **Dr**, **St**   stand for   *Mister, Mistress, Doctor, Saint.*

The rule about full stops after abbreviations is changing. Many people now do not put a full stop if the abbreviation ends with the last letter of the word:

Co. for *Company*,   **Rev**. for *Reverend*,   but **Ltd** for *Limited*.

Shorter Still

The initials **P.T.O.** stand for Please turn over.
G.M.T. stand for Greenwich Mean Time.
N.Z. stand for New Zealand.

They are called **abbreviations** because they are made brief.

It used to be the rule that a full stop was put after each initial, but we use so many of them now that it would look fussy. So in very common abbreviations we often leave the full stops out, as in BBC.

Very short words like *of* and *the* are often left out. The abbreviation of *Fellow of the Royal College of Organists* is F.R.C.O.

Write down suitable abbreviations for the following:

1. The British Medical Association
2. The Royal National Lifeboat Institution
3. The National Society for the Prevention of Cruelty to Children
4. Fellow of the Royal Geographical Society
5. Pay as you earn
6. World Health Organization

What do the following stand for?

1. CID
2. H.R.H.
3. NNW

4. EEC
5. S.R.N.
6. TUC

Who or Whom?

The policeman **who** caught the thief.

The thief **whom** the policeman caught.

The rule for **who** or **whom** is just like the rule for personal pronouns.

Subject	Object
who	whom

Use **whom** when (*a*)   it is the object of a verb,
(*b*)   it follows a preposition.

In the first sentence below the illustration, *who* refers to the policeman and is the subject of *caught*. In the second sentence *whom* refers to the thief and is the object of *caught*.

Complete the sentences below by adding correctly *who* or *whom*.

1. There is the lady _____ helped me last week.
2. There is the lady _____ I helped last week.
3. This is the farmer _____ was interviewed on television.
4. This is the farmer _____ we saw on television.

About Whom

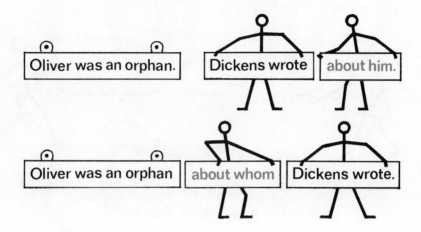

About is a preposition, so **whom** follows it.

Join these pairs of sentences, using the preposition shown in italics followed by **whom**. (You will need to change the order of the words.)

1. She is a youth leader. We go climbing *with* her.
2. The Vikings were pirates. People were afraid *of* them.
3. The picture shows a woman. A child is standing *beside* her.
4. Mr Dyer was the unlucky man. The blame fell *on* him.
5. Nelson was an admiral. Sailors put their trust *in* him.
6. Tom is a splendid chap. I have a great regard *for* him.
7. She is a pianist. I once had lessons *from* her.
8. Eiffel was an engineer. The Eiffel Tower was named *after* him.

Questions—who or whom?

1. _____ was Queen Victoria's husband?
2. _____ did you meet?
3. From _____ did you get the news?
4. _____ did you say was coming?
5. To _____ do we apply for permission?

Their Very Words

Jill said, "Look what you've done!"
"I've spilt the paint," said Jack.

In picture books and comic strips the words actually spoken are often shown in balloons. In serious printing and writing they are enclosed in quotation marks . . . "Good morning," he said.

In the two examples under the illustration, notice that . . .

The spoken words are separated from the unspoken words by a comma.

The first spoken word begins with a capital letter.

When **said** precedes the spoken words, the comma comes after **said**. When **said** follows the spoken words the comma is put before **said**, and inside the quotation marks.

Quotation marks can be a pair of double commas, or a pair of single commas:

“   ”   or   ‘   ’

They are sometimes called inverted commas.

52

Copy the sentences below in your ordinary handwriting, putting in the necessary quotation marks and other punctuation.

1. THESE ARE JAFFA ORANGES SAID THE GREENGROCER
2. THE KEEPER SAID THESE ANIMALS ARE DANGEROUS
3. YOU ARE NOT BEING VERY HELPFUL HE SAID
4. I DO NOT KNOW I ANSWERED QUICKLY
5. THE GUIDE SAID THIS PIANO WAS PLAYED BY MOZART
6. FIND OUT FOR YOURSELF WAS ALL HE WOULD SAY

When the spoken words are a question or an exclamation that mark is put inside the quotation marks and the comma is left out.

"Go away!" he shouted.   "Can you walk?" he asked.

7. HAVE YOU EVER SEEN A TEST MATCH HE ASKED
8. IS THIS THE WAY TO PLYMOUTH ASKED THE DRIVER
9. SHE SAID WHO GAVE YOU PERMISSION TO LEAVE
10. WHAT A TERRIBLE STORY SHE EXCLAIMED
11. MY MOTHER USED TO SAY PRACTICE MAKES PERFECT
12. COME BACK AT ONCE SHOUTED THE MAN

This price has been
ringed.

This bell is being
rung.

Not Their Very Words

I've lost my purse. Can you lend me some money, please?

- 3 -
She said she'd lost her purse and asked if I could lend her some money. I told

Direct Speech   Indirect Speech

Reporting words *exactly* as they were spoken is called **direct speech**. When speech is described but not quoted it is called **indirect speech**.

You will notice that in indirect speech, what the person said is usually put in the past tense.

When you are talking or writing to someone else about what others have said to you, it is often better to report the *meaning* of what was said than to repeat the actual words. This avoids having to keep on saying, "I said . . . He said . . . I said . . ." and so on.

Turn the following conversations from direct speech into indirect speech. You can avoid repeating *said* too often by using words like *told, suggested, remarked, answered, replied, exclaimed.*

1. The dentist said to me, "You have had a number of teeth stopped." I said, "Yes, six or seven."
2. Carol said, "Let's swim across to the raft." I said, "I think it's too far."
3. I said to the assistant, "The mirror you sold me is faulty." He said, "I'm sorry. If you bring it back I will replace it."
4. I said to the porter, "What time is the last train to Banbury?" He said, "The last one has gone."

54

Jim and I . . . . Jim and me

Jim and **I** tried to catch Rover.
Rover ran away from Jim and **me**.

Some people think it is always correct to say **Susan and I, my brother and I,** and so on. This is not so. We use **I** when it is the subject of a sentence, and when it completes a verb of being—**It is I. I ran.** But if it is the object of a verb or preposition we must use **me**. **It came from me. She caught me.**

The easy way of deciding whether to use **I** or **me** is to leave out the others and imagine yourself alone in the sentence.

	They invited Anna and _____.
Think:	They invited **me**.
Say:	They invited Anna and **me**.

Complete these examples with I/me or we/us.

1. _____ children had to stand.
2. There were no seats for _____ children.
3. These apples are for you and _____.
4. I'm sure you and _____ didn't leave this litter.
5. Between you and _____ it was a poor performance.
6. It's not for _____ beginners to judge.
7. Here is a photograph of Alex and _____ at Leeds.
8. Do you mind if my friend and _____ shelter here?

55

Easier to Read

> *2*
>
> Although I am fond of football cricket and tennis are the games I like best. I took 4 wickets for 37 in our match against S‑‑‑‑ Youth Club last...

Where should the writer have put a comma in the letter above? There is no strict rule for commas as there is for full stops. They should not be over-used; but they are often needed to make the meaning clear.

It is usual to put commas between words arranged in a series. **A dark, smelly, oily liquid.** (No comma is put between the last adjective and the noun.) **There were diamonds, emeralds, rubies and sapphires.** (No comma is needed before *and*.)

Something put into a sentence as explanation or additional information is separated from the rest of the sentence by commas. **Nelson, the Admiral of the Fleet, gave the order.**
James, the oldest boy in the class, came last.

In the following examples put in the necessary commas.

1. Today we had English French maths geography and science.
2. Please get sugar tea butter eggs and cheese.
3. A loud rumbling frightening noise
4. A polite cheerful helpful person
5. The weaver a small English fish has poisonous spines.
6. Alexander King of Macedon had a horse called Bucephalus.
7. Fifteen tired wet cold muddy players
8. My letter delayed in the post did not arrive in time.

All the Difference

Does this mean **Stop children from crossing** or
Stop because children are crossing?
What does this mean? **Police notice accident ahead.**
Punctuate it so that the meaning is clear.

In the following pair of sentences, which sentence means

1. *that the boy had only one hand?*
   a. A boy with only one hand saved the child from falling.
   b. A boy, with only one hand, saved the child from falling.

2. *that it was the biggest of its kind anywhere?*
   a. We saw the biggest indoor swimming pool in Montreal.
   b. We saw the biggest indoor swimming pool, in Montreal.

3. *that it is Bob who is hoping?*
   a. Father, hopes Bob, will change his mind.
   b. Father hopes Bob will change his mind.

4. *that we may not go abroad at all?*
   a. We are going abroad, perhaps to Italy.
   b. We are going abroad perhaps, to Italy.

5. *that the pedestrians are walking slowly?*
   a. Slow pedestrians crossing
   b. Slow, pedestrians crossing

Bad Habits

When speakers use incorrect or clumsy English on radio and television, their bad habits are often copied by many listeners.

Here are some undesirable examples.

1. There is a famine situation. (Omit the word *situation*.)
2. He had no alibi for losing his temper. (An *alibi* is not an excuse; it means that the person was elsewhere at the time.)
3. He was hospitalized. (Say He was in hospital.)
4. Profitwise the company has done well. (Say The company has made a good profit.)
5. At this moment in time . . . (Say At this time, or now, or at present.)
6. I am disinterested in this book. (Say not interested or uninterested. *Disinterested* means not biased, not standing to gain or lose by it.)
7. Each employee received a seasonal gift. (Say *seasonable*, meaning suitable for the season.)
8. It looks like winter is over. (Say It looks as though winter is over.)
9. I disassociate myself from what the committee is doing. (Say *dissociate*.)

Some people think they will sound more important or better educated if they use long words instead of short ones. This is not so. It is bad style to say a commodious residence when all you mean is a big house.

In most cases it is best to use straightforward language. If you must use a big word, be sure you know exactly what it means.

Rewrite the following sentences using simple language.

1. They were saddened by his decease.
2. She perused the book carefully.
3. I shall endeavour to purchase shoes to match.
4. Adverse climatic conditions prevailed.
5. He was attired in warm apparel.
6. The conflagration was expeditiously extinguished.
7. He welcomed the termination of his travail.
8. Did you receive sufficient sustenance?

 Watch out for these . . .

sort is singular, so it is wrong to say
   these sort of things are . . .
   Say this sort of thing is . . .
   or things of this sort are . . .

kind is singular too, so it is wrong to say
   those kind of things are . . .
   Say that kind of thing is . . .
   or things of that kind are

like must not be used as a conjunction. It is wrong
   to say They speak like we do.
   Say They speak like us or They speak as we do.

never Do **not** say never ever. If you want to be
   emphatic, say never, never.

Don't say: Say:
  different than   different from
  similar as   similar to

Don't Say it Twice

Just three o'clock   **or**   Exactly three o'clock
but **not**   just exactly three o'clock.

The words **just** and **exactly** mean the same.
There is no need to use them both.

In the sentences below, leave out the words that are not needed.
1. He is a wealthy millionaire.
2. She suffers from deafness in the ears.
3. The war finally ended in 1945.
4. Raise it up about ten centimetres.
5. We arrived at 5 a.m. in the morning.
6. Draw a round circle.
7. They could be reopened again.
8. You pay the subscription annually every year.
9. You will find the cheque enclosed herewith.

Express the following in two ways.
1. They crept along silently without a word.
2. We bought some old-fashioned antique furniture.
3. They found an empty box with nothing in it.
4. He was killed in a fatal accident.
5. The choir was accompanied by an orchestra of musicians.
6. We went on a little miniature railway.
7. This is a vacant house with no occupant.
8. The school had a splendid library of books.
9. She needs dental treatment for her teeth.

What are They?

Some people fight shy of the very thought of grammar. However, we can't avoid it, since we use it every time we speak. It is often convenient for us to know the right names.

In this book we have used grammatical terms only where they make it easier to understand an explanation.

Parts of Speech   is the term used for the different classes of words, e.g. nouns, verbs, conjunctions, pronouns.

The same word may occur as several different parts of speech, according to the work it is doing in each particular sentence.

This **watch** keeps good time.   (noun)
There are **watch** towers on the coast.   (adjective)
Sit still and **watch** me.   (verb)

Noun: A noun is a word that *names* something. If it names a particular thing it is a **proper** noun and must begin with a capital letter.

Jane   London   Admiral Nelson

If it names something general it is a **common** noun and does not need a capital letter.

dog   train   market

Pronoun: A pronoun is a word used instead of a noun.

you   he   they   I   it

Verb: A verb tells what the subject of a sentence does, what is done to the subject of a sentence, or it expresses the state of the subject.

The man **fell** to the ground.
The man **was thrown** to the ground.
The man **was** on the ground.

61

Verbs can be **active** when the subject does the action, or **passive** if the action is done to the subject.

> He **fell** to the ground.   (active)
>
> He **was thrown** to the ground.   (passive)

Verbs are called **transitive** if the action directly affects an object. Verbs are **intransitive** if the action or state affects only the subject.

> The monkey **ate** the banana.   (transitive)
>
> The monkey **was eating**.   (intransitive)

A verb may be expressed in one word, or it may require several words.

> He sang.
> He is singing.
> He has been singing.

Participle: A participle is an incomplete verb. Together with one or more helping verbs it can form a complete verb. It can be used on its own as an adjective.

The present participle always ends in **-ing**.

> I am **speaking**.   (used as a verb)
> The **speaking** clock.   (used as an adjective)

Past participles very often end in **-ed**, **-d**, or **-t**,

> walked   tasted   kept

or in **-en**, **-n**,

> spoken   known
> I have **spoken** —verb.
> The **spoken** word —adjective.

Adjective: An adjective is a word that describes or limits a noun.

> **Swiss** watches   a **clever** child   **this** book

Adverb: An adverb tells more about a verb, or modifies an adjective or adverb.

She ran **swiftly**.
It was **very** slippery.
She spoke **rather** fast.

Conjunction: A conjunction is a word that joins two words, phrases or sentences. Conjunctions can be single words **and as** or groups of words **as well as neither . . . nor.**

Preposition: A preposition governs a noun or pronoun and relates it to something else.

The hat is on the table.
On governs **table** and relates it to **hat**.

INDEX OF CONTENTS